Irrefutable

My Proof for the Law of Attraction

SEEMA T. CHANDARANA

BALBOA.
PRESS

A DIVISION OF HAY HOUSE

Balboa Press books may be ordered through booksellers or by contacting:

Balboa Press
A Division of Hay House
1663 Liberty Drive
Bloomington, IN 47403
www.balboapress.com
1-(877) 407-4847

Because of the dynamic nature of the Internet, any web addresses or links contained in this book may have changed since publication and may no longer be valid. The views expressed in this work are solely those of the author and do not necessarily reflect the views of the publisher, and the publisher hereby disclaims any responsibility for them.

The author of this book does not dispense medical advice or prescribe the use of any technique as a form of treatment for physical, emotional, or medical problems without the advice of a physician, either directly or indirectly. The intent of the author is only to offer information of a general nature to help you in your quest for emotional and spiritual well-being. In the event you use any of the information in this book for yourself, which is your constitutional right, the author and the publisher assume no responsibility for your actions.

Any people depicted in stock imagery provided by Thinkstock are models, and such images are being used for illustrative purposes only.
Certain stock imagery © Thinkstock.

ISBN: 978-1-4525-7279-6 (sc)
ISBN: 978-1-4525-7280-2 (e)

Library of Congress Control Number: 2013907181

Printed in the United States of America.

Balboa Press rev. date: 05/21/2013

For those who want to believe
that the Law of Attraction works infallibly
and are still searching for more proof

Words do not teach. It is life experience that brings you your knowing. And so we encourage you to reflect into your own life experience to remember those things that you have experienced before and to begin watching from this point forward for the absolute correlation between the . . . [thoughts you are thinking] . . . and the life experience that you are living, for it is our knowing that there is not a shred of evidence that exists anywhere in your universe that is to the contrary of [the Law of Attraction].

—Abraham, *The Law of Attraction*

Contents

Preface

You create your own reality.
—Seth, *The Seth Material*

The inspiration for this collection of stories came from what I lovingly call my Bible, the book by Abraham-Hicks entitled *Ask and It Is Given*. Abraham jests that the title rivals all titles of all time, and that reading the title is all that is necessary to understand the content. My enthusiasm for its message came at just the moment I needed to hear it, however. Had I read the book any sooner, it may have just pissed me off as I'm sure it does those who aren't ready to hear. Hear what, you ask? *You are the creator of your own experiences.* All of them. The good, the bad, and the ugly. All day, every day, life causes us to ask for things—for more clarity, more joy, more peace, more alignment, more! When we line up with it, life feels delicious. When we complain about what is, we buck up against what naturally wants to flow to us: everything we desire.

We may find it easy to apply this theory of how life works when we notice things working out well for us, but for those seemingly unfortunate circumstances for which we contend, "I didn't ask for *this*!" it may be more difficult to accept that we are the sole creator of our life. I didn't ask for disease. I didn't ask for divorce. I didn't ask for unemployment. I didn't ask for mold in my basement. And I get that. I understand how it could be difficult to see that hidden within those unfortunate circumstances are the answers to all we have asked for. So I have written and shared my stories to show that no matter the situation, wanted or unwanted, in every case the outcome was a direct result of my thinking.

Each time I find myself focusing on something in my life I would rather experience differently, I sit down to write another story, and doing so affirms my faith in the universal law, "Ask and it is given," once again. What I appreciate the most about understanding how the law works is that there are no exceptions to it (hence the term law). I love its predictability! I love that when I dress myself well in the morning and walk out the door confidently and feeling pretty, I inevitably receive compliments the whole day through. I love that when I even silently curse the driver in front of me on the way to the store, I find myself in the checkout line with the rudest of clerks. I love knowing that what I put out there comes right back to me, and when I put out what I want, I get back what is wanted. Isn't this the Golden Rule? Surprisingly enough, however, it endears me just as much to know that when I put out bad vibes, things go wrong for me too. This discovery was so empowering! After all, if I could create crap, imagine what I could create if I really put my mind to it!

So this book is a collection of my personal stories, the evidence of how the Law of Attraction works in my life. They are my stories of creation—unconscious creations, unwanted creations, and yes, occasionally even some deliberate creations. I rejoice in sharing all these creations with you, for at times they highlight how events transpired almost mystically and magically, and at other times how they unfolded quite unpleasantly for myself and others. Every time, however, the events unfolded predictably, and what a palpable power there is in that! In this puzzle of connecting the dots from what happens in my life back to the thoughts and beliefs I carry with me daily, I was able to see how I am the creator of my own experience, the good, the bad, and the ugly. The all of it.

I feel I should offer a few words on the daily affirmations I list at the beginning of each chapter. Each one is either a direct quote from the guru of affirmations, Louise L. Hay, or one that I have adapted to fit for me personally. I created a blessed and fortunate opportunity, which you'll also read about in this book, to work with her in an intimate workshop on crafting positive affirmations. As a result, I have become extremely aware of every statement I think, speak, and write, for as Louise puts it, "Everything is an affirmation." The consistency of practicing the affirmations from her daily calendar has permeated my mind and my consciousness with such positive thoughts that this language has simply become my way of speech now, and while I have attempted unsuccessfully to trace the source of each affirmation I present in this book, I credit even the ones I could not find in print to the work Louise has shared with us. Admittedly, not all of these statements were practiced thoughts for me prior to the unfolding of the events in each story you'll read, but I can assure you that if I wasn't practicing the affirmations before that time, I am certainly practicing them now! Abraham teaches that when we continue to think a thought, that thought develops into what we call a belief. The mathematician in me sees a certain logic, then, in inserting a new thought about how I would like things to be, and then practicing it long enough until I actually believe it. Soon enough, reality reflects back my beliefs, and I realize a miracle has occurred: I have created my own reality.

But don't take my word for it. Try it out for yourself! I encourage you to look at your own stories to find evidence of the law at work. I have confidence you won't have to search too far back as the law is ineffable. In all my years of searching, I cannot find one example of an exception to the law. Sometimes the answers are disguised and sometimes they are obvious, and in every case they are a direct result of my thoughts. I hope my stories inspire you to find meaning behind the twists, turns, and seemingly unexpected events in your life. Nothing is an accident, and nothing can come into our experience without our invitation. Once we own that, we're sitting in the driver's seat on our way to a place of infinite possibilities!

So buckle up. here we go!

Chapter 1

KCT 17

Daily Affirmation #1:

"My life is unfolding in perfect divine order."

*M*y name is Seema Trivedi Chandarana. At least, now it is. And likely it will always be. You see, like many other middle-aged women who have left a marriage behind, I have had two last names, but what makes me unique is that I have also had three middle names. This is where my story begins.

At my birth, I was given the name Seema Kantilal Chandarana. When I was growing up in a mostly white neighborhood, the name Seema was a blessing since it was easy to pronounce and phonetic in spelling. My brother, Anand, converted his name to Andy, while my mother, Paragini, used the pseudonym Peggy, and my father, Kantilal, took on the identity of Ken, although he was the furthest thing from a male Barbie doll. My mom tried to call me Sam or Samantha on occasion, to make me "fit in" with my own family, but it never took, as the name Seema (or Seems or Seemers to those closest to me) took to me really well. It even turned out that when calling to order Chinese food for takeout, Dad would shorten our last name to Chan, as though we ought to have been cooking Chinese food at home. So much wrapped up in a name. It's no wonder I've changed it twice and have received at least six different permutations of it in my junk mail.

Now, if you've got an eye for details you'll notice that my middle name was the same as my father's first name. It's not because he adored me more than anything else in the world. You see, my brother's name is Anand Kantilal Chandarana, my mother's name is Paragini Kantilal Chandarana, and we even joked that if our dog had a birth certificate, it would have read Sparky Kantilal Chandarana. The Hindu tradition is very patriarchal by nature, and between each first and middle name, I can hear a little whisper of the word "of"—Seema "of" Kantilal Chandarana, Paragini "of" Kantilal Chandarana, Anand "of" Kantilal Chandarana, in case you ever forget to whom you belong, as though we were all property of my father. As a young girl, I simply hated having a boy's name as my middle name. Every girl I knew had some sweet, easy middle name like Beth, Lynn, or Grace. As a woman, I realize now that this name given to me at birth lit the first little flame under my inner feminist's pants.

So, when I got married, I could hardly wait to dump my middle name. Problem was, according to tradition, my middle name would be replaced from my father's first name to my husband's first name. When hell froze over! Now, my husband-to-be had a last name only one letter shy of the number of letters in Chandarana, and the thought of a hyphenated last name containing twenty characters was more than I could bear. It seemed that the right way to maintain my sense of identity when entering this joint merger was to replace my middle name with my last name. Finally, there would be no gap between the Seema and the Chandarana.

Fast-forward eight years to the dissolution of my marriage, and so much of the foundation of my life, and you'll see a young woman searching yet again for a name that fit all that she had become. Nearly a year had passed, and I still found myself signing my married name. On a long weekend in Madrid visiting a friend, I paid the credit card bill after tapas one evening, and on the walk home, my friend opened the discussion of my name. "I don't understand you Americans, changing your name when you get married. We are given a name at birth and we keep it until death. It's who you are, and who you are doesn't change, so why should your name?"

That conversation, and my romanticism for all things Spanish, led me to contemplate the perfect nature of the naming system in this culture. Your mother and father choose a beautiful first and middle name for you (only they're not so much like Beth, Lynn, or Grace but more like Isabel, Mercedes, or Graciela), and then you are awarded both your father's surname and your mother's surname. What a beautiful way to honor both parents equally (this pleases my inner feminist very much)! Another added benefit of this naming system is that it allows a person to trace back a family tree as far and as widely as possible, letting that person know each generation's paternal and maternal heritage. Even better, every form you fill out in your life time has a space for all four of your names! Our culture has not managed to be quite so accommodating yet.

Our conversation stayed with me all the way back to the States, and it stewed in my heart for a few more months until it finished cooking during a weekend I drove out to Iowa. I was on my way to the Raj for my first panchakarma cleanse. The Raj is an amazing Ayurveda retreat center in Fairfield, Iowa, where the Maharishi set up camp. You know, the one that The Beatles studied with, the one George flew to India to see and came back all enlightened and such. Yes, the Maharishi was quite a sage, a genius devoted to the science of being, and a master at the art of living. His legacy has left us with a completely *sattvic* community (in the middle of corn rows) where all the buildings face east to welcome the morning sun, and the entire community stops to meditate twice daily. This was the place for me to learn how to live my best life, and I felt at home surrounded by a community of yogis versed in both Sanskrit and the ancient teachings of India.

As it came to pass, the lady behind the reception desk commented on my last name, Chandarana, with wonder and delight. "Goddess of the Moon! What a great name." This might have been the first time in my life I had not translated my name for a fellow American—these people got it right away. Ha! I decided to have a little fun with that and told the gal that my mom's maiden name was "Trivedi." Then, I saw it happen, what my favorite *masi*, my mom's sister, had been telling me about for so long. A certain air of reverence and respect came over the receptionist, and as her demeanor changed, so did mine. You see, Trivedi stands for three (tri) Vedas, as in Ayur-Veda. My mother's, and hence my own heritage is Brahmin, a priestly caste of people who are well versed in the ancient sacred teachings. The name Trivedi was awarded after having mastered the first three Vedas, thus deeming the person with it liable for teaching the public these Vedas' contents. The way the people there looked at me and treated me was unlike anything I had known before. The respect that I saw reflected back in them awakened a dormant part of who I was at my core. And on my drive home, my name finally came to me as a mix of my wannabe Spanish roots and my actual Indian roots: Seema Trivedi Chandarana.

But that's not where the story ends. Shortly after my name change was legal and officially on my driver's license, I was driving with a friend who innocently asked, "Seema, what's your middle name?" She then heard the whole crazy story straight from my own lips. I was laughing as I told it, amused that anyone could go through so many derivations on the same few words. Still, I didn't piece it all together until it all came together one night in a dream. I dreamed of my license plate, which reads KCT 17. Friends had asked me for years what it meant, as though it were a vanity plate I had requested when buying my minivan. It seemed as though it could be. After all, the numbers and letters look like initials followed by a favorite number. But they weren't my initials, at least not at the time, nor are they now. What they are, however, are each of my middle initials, in the order in which I received them. That license plate was issued to me, and in so many ways I believe as well that my stories were too.

What then is the meaning of the 17, you wonder? I wondered for years too, until I realized that all I had to do was ask. So I put the question out there and settled on the idea that when the answer came, this collection of stories would be complete. The book you hold in your hands is the evidence that we are always answered, so keep reading . . . everything is unfolding perfectly for you!

Chapter 2

When in Doubt, Take a Taxi

Daily Affirmation #2:

"I am always in the right place, at the right time, doing the right thing."

The title of this chapter appears on a long list of "Things I Learned" while spending a semester studying abroad. It's a story that takes place in Florence, Italy, but starts back in Champaign, Illinois. A sorority sister of mine had applied to study art in Newcastle upon Tyne, England. It made sense; she was an art major. To me, studying abroad sounded exotic, exciting, exuberant! I wanted a little piece of that, but I was enrolled as a mathematics major then. In fact, I graduated as a mathematics major. So it didn't seem I had much business in the study abroad office, except I've already mentioned my love of all things Spanish, haven't I?

My friend, Sandy, had left sometime in late August, to go abroad for the entire school year. Mind you, this was back before the days of cell phones and reliable and readily accessible internet. E-mail was just emerging, and after registering at the university, I shamefully trashed the notice regarding my e-mail account with other seemingly useless papers. It required some investigation to activate my idle account, but I had a great desire to keep connected to my friend. Once my account was established, I voraciously read about her escapades, living vicariously through her novel adventures, and she drew upon the familiarity of my tales of barhopping to stave off any homesickness that might have crept in. As the days grew colder and darker, I grew more and more ready to hop on a plane to the "Florida of Europe," and when I finally landed, I seemed so close to where my friend was that I immediately set into motion plans to meet up with her.

At that time, the Universidad de Granada had three computers for all of the students to use, and I remember waiting in line for up to an hour sometimes just for a few moments to check my account. Despite the technological obstructions, Sandy and I finally made plans to see each other. It just so happened that the week I would have a break from classes was the same week her class would be on a field trip to study art in Florence, Italy. The timing was perfect! And although we didn't have many (or any) of the details worked out, she did send the address of the hostel her school had booked and the date they planned to arrive. I guess we figured we'd just take it from there.

As I emerged from the airport in Florence, I sat down on my suitcase to get my bearings. I noticed a bright orange bus (it was kind of hard not to notice it, actually) and drew upon old memories of having visited Italy with my parents back in grade school. Dad was a fan of learning the public transport systems when we traveled. It saved money and helped us blend in with the locals, or whatever. My Spanish was improving after six weeks immersed in the culture, and Italian is also a romantic language. Perhaps I could figure out where the bus was headed, where the hostel was in town, and how close I could get to there, I thought. I nearly had it all put together, and in the same moment, that bus pulled away. Of course, I was still sitting on my suitcase, and when I came out of my head long enough to notice the bus had left, I decided to take a taxi instead.

I handed the taxi driver a printout of the email Sandy had sent me, and he nodded, zipping away through the traffic. Were we headed north? South? Into the city? In circles? At this point, all my faith, and my fare, were in his hands. He delivered me to a nine-foot solid wood door, and when no one answered the ring of the bell, I made my way inside. A portly old Italian woman greeted me, and that's when I figured out all the Spanish I learned in textbooks at home and during my weeks in Granada wasn't going to get me very far in Italy. So I thanked her kindly as she motioned me over to the couch in the waiting room. Although she too had seen the e-mail I had printed out, I still searched for a business card or letterhead or something to confirm that I was truly in the right place, on the right day, at the right time . . . and that's when two men, speaking very broken Italian, came in to check in with the signora. I hesitantly approached them asking, "Do you speak English?" I was delighted by their response of, "Are you looking for Sandy?"

They led me down to the street where a great big charter bus was waiting, and out rushed my friend with open arms and a little squeal of joy. Oh to see a familiar face of a good friend in a foreign land! She then began to tell her tales of woe: an alarm clock that failed, a missed bus, a phone call to America in panic, and her determined mother who said, and I quote, "Sandy, you do what you have to. Seema will be there waiting for you." (Thank you, Mrs. J!) She had taken a train to race the bus to the English Channel to catch up with her group and pulled into the ferry dock just moments before it sailed away.

Our reunion played out like a scene in a movie, and if there were ever a moment in my life to define the word "glee," this was it. It was as though all of the forces in this time-space reality had conspired to bring the perfect alignment of details together so I could be standing on that sidewalk in Florence hugging my dear friend at just the moment we both needed it most. I really didn't think it could get any better than that, until it did.

When we decided to meet there on that day, we still hadn't ironed out where I would stay. You see, Sandy was there on an excursion with her school group. The charter bus and accommodations were all part of the package deal. Me, I was more like a stowaway, happy to tag along and take up as little floor space as possible for the night, or on the more luxurious side of things, hoping to rent an extra room at the same hostel for the duration. As it turned out, the day before the group set off, one of the girls had come down with mononucleosis. Of course, she was unable to travel, and as it turned out, she was also slotted to bunk in Sandy's room. So there it was, an open, prepaid bed waiting just for me.

I think this was the first time I noticed the forces greater than me at work. It wasn't our e-mails or our intentions to meet up that made every detail of our coming together happen so seamlessly. It was a conspiring for the greatest good of everyone involved that orchestrated a perfect unfolding of events, and it seemed that was just the tip of the iceberg.

Thank you, Universe!

Chapter 3

Three is the Magic Number

Daily Affirmation #3:

"Every hand that touches me is a healing hand."
—Louise Hay, *Heart Thoughts*

My belly had finally "popped," and using a rubber band to hold my jeans together gave way to maternity jeans. In the sixteenth week of my first pregnancy, I could no longer hide the evident bulge of my expanding bump. It seemed that as quickly as the excitement over showcasing my condition in cutely tailored fashions designed just for that purpose had come over me, it rapidly washed away. The rubber band on the jeans was replaced by the tight sensation of a rubber band stretching behind my navel—my abdominal muscles, to be specific. And it itched! Only no amount of scratching on the outside would relieve the discomfort inside. Weekly updates on my baby's growth comparing it to the size of a fruit each time—an olive by week eight, a lemon by week twelve, a mango by week sixteen—left me 1) hungry and 2) with a heavy feeling, as though my pelvic bowl were more like a fruit bowl. But the final straw was the tightness in my chest as my ribs held tight to their mission of protecting such soft and vulnerable organs, failing to release enough to accommodate our new resident.

That's when I decided that massage no longer fit the category of luxury; rather, it became a necessity. I asked for a reference from the one person I trusted to know about the body, my yoga teacher, and she gave me two. The first of the referrals offered what I interpreted as standard body massage, and the other promoted craniosacral therapy, which I knew nothing about at the time. So I phoned a friend who had recently graduated from massage school for her opinion. Her response still fills me with laughter today: "I *hate* those people! I can never figure out how they do what they do, and it's so amazing!" The envy in my studied and trusted friend was enough for me to consider the option, but truly, I'm not certain why I deliberated for so long. I could hardly ignore the divine pushes toward this work as the gal who offered the craniosacral therapy lived on the next block from me!

That winter I donned my warm woolies and walked through the snow down the street for six weekly, consecutive sessions. Birds chirped, squirrels scurried about, and the quiet of Sunday afternoons prepared me for what would come next. I remember being in tears when I told her why I had sought her out, that with five more months of pregnancy remaining, I could barely imagine making any more room in my body for my baby to grow. She set the intention to allow more space and focused her mind and energy on accomplishing this goal as we set off to do the work on her table. I also remember remaining fully clothed while her hands simply hovered over my body. I understood my friend's strong reaction to this type of work and could hear skeptical thoughts pass through my mind, but it was easy to dismiss them, focusing instead on the beautiful blue of her massage room, staying open to possibilities. The perfect conditions for sprouting a miracle were set, and that's exactly what happened.

Exhaling slowly, I felt each vertebrae in my spine extend. It seemed that I had grown an inch taller! I didn't have a moment to marvel in the sensation before she said aloud, "Good, just like that," and I thought, "Just like what? How does she know what I'm feeling when her hands aren't even touching me?" It didn't matter though. The shift had already happened, and her work for that session was complete. When I expressed my concern that coming off the table and standing vertically might compress my vertebrae back to their original form, she lovingly assured me that it would not happen, today or ever. And she was right.

In subsequent sessions, I experienced the same synchronicity of feeling relief coordinated with her verbal expression of praise. Once, she laid her hands over me and helped to open up my pelvic cavity. The next day I felt lighter, and all day long people commented on how round my belly seemed, as I could feel that the baby now lay cradled lower in my pelvis, which now felt more like a snuggly bassinet than a fruit bowl! In another session we worked on my rib cage, and I kid you not—I could not fasten my bra in the morning! Luckily, I discovered I could purchase a little bra extender to add two more inches around, and I still marvel at how quickly the work took effect.

She informed me after our last session that she was packing up to move to Florida. In the white of our winter, I bid her a joyous farewell even though a part of me longed for more of her work. But I sensed we had completed our work together, and that I would make it through until the end, which incidentally ended up being forty-*one* weeks of pregnancy! Although I haven't seen her since, I carry with me all the profound effects of her work to this day.

Fast-forwarding to some months later, I stumbled into a yoga studio with my colicky newborn for a seminar with a lactation consultant. We didn't have problems nursing, but we certainly had problems that were beyond my ability to cope with at the time. I felt pulled to go there and was not sure why I went until I met Judy. Something so familiar and warm in her eyes reassured me everything would improve and help was on the way.

"Would you be open to alternative therapies?" she probed me.

Desperate for relief, I said, "Sure, why not?" and had a good chuckle, for the first time in a while, when she referred me to a craniosacral therapist.

The sessions with my second miracle worker proved to be equally amazing, but for various and sundry reasons, our work together got cut short. In part I made excuses that her office was too far, that my schedule was too full, that the therapy didn't really effect great change, but ultimately it was my own subconscious belief that I didn't deserve to feel good that kept me from getting the treatments from her that I needed. Time passed, and I moved to a new home. Then after two years, I became pregnant for the second time, and I had an instant flash of desire to seek this woman out. For me, the second time around for anything, this time being pregnancy, usually feels tinged with a competitive edge; I want to do it better than the first and have a certain power of wisdom and hindsight to work from. I dug out her old business card and made a call to her, but I never got a response.

At first, I was dismayed, maybe even annoyed; but having experienced the miraculous shifts in my first pregnancy, I was determined to have the same thing happen again. So a few months later, I put all doubts, fears, and judgments aside and called the number again. This time she answered, and as we chatted, I learned that she had never gotten my first message. Looking back, I can see that my own thoughts of unworthiness blocked my message from going through. At that point, I didn't believe I deserved to "splurge" on such indulgences. This time, however, as my belly "popped" again and the familiar twinges of constrained panic bubbled up, I knew deeply that our treatments were a vital component of my prenatal care. It would follow naturally then that this time she answered the call. I eagerly booked a session with her for that week when she informed me she had moved her work location. Paying no mind to such a small detail, I agreed to meet her wherever she practiced, and to my delight, her space happened to be one mile from my new home!

Our work continued for years, yielding great results as well, until one day she announced she was moving to Colorado. Now, I can't say what prompts my healers to leave Chicago (okay, maybe it's the harsh winters), but I do believe the universe abhors a vacuum. The empty space this time drew in my third miracle healer, who isn't a craniosacral therapist by trade. He is a chiropractor. Okay, still a doctor for the spine, so almost the same thing!

Herein lies the core of my message to you for this chapter. Healing is as natural a process as breathing. I have seen half my cherry tree struck down to the ground by a storm only to flourish and bear fruit the following season. When in a state of disease, our positive thoughts and images of health can certainly aid the natural process of healing, but even this may not be necessary. I have come to learn from angel experts like Doreen Virtue and Sonia Choquette that healing guides are continually paving a direct path to health for us to follow. For me, it's usually a path signed by three landmarks. The closer together they appear in time, the more clearly I can follow.

This time around, I got my three signals in the course of a short week. The first was delivered on Tuesday night when my yoga teacher, after nine months of working on backbends with me, suggested I see a chiropractor about a collapsing vertebra. The second came from a coworker who overheard me talking about my aforementioned colicky baby and offered that a friend of his had success relieving some of the colic symptoms with a chiropractor. The third came from a headline on the front page of a newspaper. I can't even recall the story, but that the word "chiropractor" leaped off the page and landed directly into my Being. It's a moment like that when I have complete faith that when we ask, we are always answered, and sometimes we are answered even when we don't ask.

Chapter 4

Like Cogs in a Wheel

Daily Affirmation #4:

"When the time is right for a new job, the perfect job finds me."

I graduated with a degree in education, and I did it before I could legally buy liquor. Skipping fifth grade as a kid and entering college with sophomore status made me too young yet to live out my heart's desire: teaching high schoolers. Having only a few years on some of the senior students, and all of those years spent in the confines of a classroom, I decided to equip myself with knowledge beyond that offered in our educational system before stepping in front of a chalkboard—Yes, that's what we still used to teach with back then!—in front of eager young minds, so similar to mine at the time. So when the university awarded me my papers, I set out on a corporate path to explore the working world a bit before returning to the hallowed halls.

I landed a position in sales working for a grocery company that had ranked on the Fortune 500 list since before time began, and the people I worked with fostered my growth beyond my expectations. I often say that those were great years to "grow up" a bit, make some mistakes, and learn my way around the professional world. But after a few years, my heart started pounding for my attention again. The time approached quickly for me to make my move back into education.

Of course, I saw no urgent reason to leave my current position. At the age of twenty-four, I had a company car, a company computer, a travel budget, an expense account, and a work-from-home flexibility second to none. I simply did the work of envisioning a life in the classroom, the satisfaction of creative lessons to inspire curiosity, the gratitude of affecting change in American youth, and I bided my time. Truthfully, the solution came more quickly than I expected. Within a few months of working on my new vision, I had landed a position in one of the top school districts in the area and signed a contract for the following school year on the day before Thanksgiving!—ten months before my first day on the job. Then, I wondered how I might stick it out at my current sales position for the duration.

As it would happen, I got transferred to a local account in Chicago that required far less travel than my previous assignment. At the same time, a townhome I had set my sights on months earlier came on the market. After a bit of creative financing, I became a proud first-time homeowner, and slowly I climbed up a steep learning curve of figuring out how things work, or rather more like how things didn't work. I immersed myself in the activities of nesting in my new home and planning the details of my wedding gala, all the while enjoying the luxury of a full-time salary and flexible hours spent "working" at home. While occasional misgivings arose over wanting more time to work on my home and wedding plans than on my account, I swiftly brushed them aside.

Behind the scenes, bigger changes were in the works. Rumor had it that a national corporation had plans to buy out our local account, and with the acquisition, they intended to release all the current sales force—namely, me. Now, this set off a panic in most of what we called the "lifers" who I worked with, but I was already one foot out the door. So no one was cheering (silently on the inside) more than I! What a perfect transition, and what perfect timing. My hearts' desires were all materializing, and my faith in the workings of the universe could hardly have been any stronger than right in that moment, until what happened next.

As happens with each of my stories, things only got better from there. You see, I was young and had potential for growth within the company. So they asked me to stay on, to trust they would reposition me to another account of my choosing. But in the meantime, for the sake of legal fairness, they were bound to offer me a severance package of two months' salary. Ha! Perfect timing and a parting gift.

Thank you (again), Universe!

Chapter 5

An Equal Exchange

Daily Affirmation #5:

"I deserve the best, and I accept the best now."
—Louise Hay, *Life! Reflections on Your Journey*

llow me to set the scene: eleven weeks after having given birth for the first time, my return date to work encroached upon my recovery from the event and the transition into a new role as a mother. Unbeknownst to me, childbirth can be a traumatic event, one in which I nearly died on the table. Of course, none of the doctors wanted to admit that due to the fear of a malpractice lawsuit. So, my feelings left me confused about the actual events, and my mind did all it could to cope—which meant developing post-traumatic stress disorder around the memory. The craziest part about all of that for me was that everyone's favorite question—friends, family and strangers alike—was, "How was the birth?", and this triggered a sense of imminent death for my psyche each time.

Oh yeah, I had gone loony. Only I didn't really know it. I did know enough, however, to return to work on a part-time basis. And for the most part, I managed it. Being up three times every night with my baby for seven straight months (the baby suffered from traumatic events as well) left us both sleep deprived. After the 4 a.m. feeding, I would place my baby back to sleep in the car seat so we could leave the house by six thirty. One commute and two classes later, I could relieve the sitter from the baby's colic cries. Some days I look back and wonder how we made it through, but we did.

So when my boss approached proposing that I pick up another class in my work load, it seemed like a good idea. I'm joking. Really. Therein lies the proof that I was mentally impaired.

Just five days into the new routine, my body began to drag my spirit around. If you ran a search for the term "walking dead," my picture might have been posted there. But one day while attempting to nurse my baby for our afternoon nap, I heard screams so loud that it completely shook me up inside. I had lost my milk completely, and the baby was hungry.

I can guess what you might be thinking . . . formula, first foods, something else to eat perhaps? Over time I have certainly evolved into a more Earth-loving, eco-conscious, all-natural kind of modern-day hippie of sorts, but the fact that my baby would only drink from the breast was not a conscious choice on my part. I enlisted all kinds of specialists to help with bottle feeding, without any success. My least favorite response came from the hospital nurse: "Hm! I've never met a baby just a few days old that could tell the difference between a nipple and the breast. What a smart baby!" And my most favorite response came from my lactation consultant, Judy, who descended from heaven above to assist me: "Your baby needs you, and your place is together, for now." She prescribed us lots of time cuddling in bed, cosleeping, massive amounts of water, and heavy doses of fenugreek to increase the milk supply, and within forty-eight hours, we got our groove back on.

One thing was clear for certain to me from that experience: the third class I had picked up needed to go. I immediately phoned by boss to let her know that a replacement had to be found as soon as possible. I had bitten off more than I could chew, or digest, like a vegetarian attempting to eat a one-pound burger. I needed to restore balance again, and quickly.

By the end of the week, a replacement had been found. In the meantime, the class was a disaster. I take full credit for that. I had no capacity to plan for the days, or learn the students' names. I served as a warm body, as we call it, in the classroom, an adult on the premises in the event of an emergency, but the students' teacher . . . that I was not.

So, when my next paycheck came, feelings of lack, shame, and insufficiency came over me. How could they have even considered paying me for what I had *not* done for them? I gave them my worst, and they gave me four hundred dollars for it. I deposited the money into my account, but without any joy or appreciation.

I didn't think much of the whole incident until a few weeks later when I was driving home from work around lunchtime. On a whim, I decided to call a friend to meet up for lunch. Doing the most responsible thing I could think of, I pulled into a nearby gas station to phone my friend. We decided on a restaurant, and I hung up. I put my minivan in reverse, winked at my baby, and had begun to back up when I heard that scrape and crunch of metal that always sounds so much louder from the inside of the car, especially when it comes from my own! I stopped. I exited. I remained surprisingly calm.

A young driver emerged from his truck. The truck was low, and it had nearly exited the gas station to the left of me, as I looked over my right shoulder and began to back up. We both acknowledged immediately that he would have been in a complete blind spot for me, and that this had truly been an accident. I appreciated his generous benefit of the doubt, and perhaps the sight of my baby in the car and the months of sleep deprivation in my eyes opened his compassionate heart to me. So we sat on the curb and deliberated on a fair solution to our dilemma.

He immediately offered that we leave the car insurance companies out of it, as my deductible would increase and the damage was minor, likely less than my deductible. He also offered that a few friends of his who worked in auto-body repair could probably get his car fixed for a less than market price. After some brief mental calculations, we agreed on a two hundred dollar settlement. I wrote him a check on the spot, and we exchanged phone numbers in the event that we needed to contact each other again regarding the incident.

At lunch that day, I relayed the story to my friend, counting one blessing after another. Nobody had been hurt. The damage to my minivan was negligible. He was willing to settle, and for less than what was fair really. Then I could feel it in my gut . . . an uncomfortable feeling of discord, a question of whether the situation were still incomplete, a concern that more repercussions were coming. Those thoughts were hanging over us like an umbrella when my cell phone rang. It was the young driver. He had called some friends, got some more opinions, researched more about what would be needed to repair his truck, and he wanted more money from me. I suppose I could feel it coming, from the moment I pulled out of the gas station. But an interesting twist came next: when he mentioned how much more money he needed, I knew that the matter would be done for good. I knew without a doubt that the whole situation had unfolded so perfectly to teach me such a priceless lesson that would change how I valued myself from that day forward. I knew our meeting was no accident because he asked me for two hundred dollars more, and the sum of what I would pay out (and I paid it) was four hundred, the exact amount for which I felt completely undeserving.

I came to know in that moment that the universe doesn't play favorites. It doesn't discern between thoughts of wanted things and thoughts of unwanted things. It simply and fairly responds to each thought equally. Through my feelings of lack, shame, and insufficiency, I sent out a signal that I didn't deserve the money and the universe responded in kind, taking it all right back from me. Even now as I write these words, gratitude wells up in my core for the invaluable insight I gained through this experience and the newborn desire to continue practicing this daily affirmation more in my life.

Chapter 6

Boomerang

Daily Affirmation #6:

"I send love out into the world and it returns to me multiplied."

The Bible says, "You reap what you sow," which I suppose sums up the law of karma in just five words. This Biblical phrase also echoes the idea "Ask and it is given" when considering the definite relationship between what we think about and what we get. This story is really not about me, but rather about my mother, and one I experienced as a witness to the power of the law in action.

It begins on the streets of London—Oxford Avenue to be specific—on a mother-daughter shopping spree. The year was 1995, and we were on holiday together after my semester in Spain, staying with some friends in town. With a pair of shoes for each of us in tow, we approached the sales counter to check out. Mom took out her credit card to pay, tucking her clutch under her arm, and as we chatted happily with the clerk, Mom suddenly noticed that her clutch had vanished. The clerk alerted security right away, to no avail, as crowds bustled around us and the thief disappeared into the scene.

I remember all of these events well, and I suppose it was a pretty typical tourist nightmare. But in writing this story, I asked my mom for her memory of the events, and what she recalls in vivid detail impresses me. She remembers we had left our passports behind, and so very luckily we could still fly home without a glitch. She remembers there had been about two hundred dollars and fifty pounds in cash in her wallet, proudly boasting that her new shoes were the most expensive pair she ever wore, and swelling with gratitude that the security office at the store had given us twenty pounds in cash to take a cab back to our friends' home. She remembers she had photos of herself and me, along with photos of Ganesh and Shankar, two of her favorite Hindu gods. She remembers a little slip of paper with the address of a sister of one of her friends who was living in Stockholm at the time, scratched down at the last minute in case there was time to hop over for a visit. (Mom had been known to do things like that!) And this one is my favorite: she remembers a receipt from a Chinese restaurant we ate at. A memory like an elephant, I tell you!

Fast-forward eight years to a dinner party near Chicago. The same friend whose sister was still living in Stockholm had recently returned from a visit abroad. She pulled my mom into the next room and asked if a clutch she had could possibly be hers. Imagine the surprise on my mom's face . . . and the confusion on her friend's! Shocked to see this little wallet after so many years, my mom opened it up to find all the contents still inside, down to the last rusty penny and the Chinese food receipt.

After mom retold the story there and then to her friend, her friend continued it. It turns out that shortly after the incident at the store, the police had found the clutch, perhaps in a garbage dumpster, perhaps turned in by a Good Samaritan. One can only speculate. Going through the purse, they contacted the only person they could: my mom's friend's sister in Stockholm. She confessed that she hadn't been near London in years and that the wallet did not belong to her. But since they didn't know what else to do with it, they shipped it off to her in Sweden. She had been quite ill during these years, and although she had been in close contact with her sister in Chicago frequently, their conversations barely had a chance to touch upon such chance things. Until somehow during that visit in 2003 when she showed the wallet to her visiting sister, who opened it, recognized the old photo of my mom and brought it back home to be safely returned to its rightful owner.

Of course, like all stories, this one gets even better, because this little miracle was not the first one my mom conjured up! Back in 1986, the two of us had flown to India together on Christmas Eve to visit my great-grandmother. I remember that she was sick, and this would be our last visit to see her. My mom insisted, rightfully so, that we have some photos taken—four generations of our family together—documenting our family history in the making. With the mission accomplished, we headed back through Heathrow Airport to fly home when at some point my mom realized she had left the rolls of film behind, four of them in a Ziploc bag with nothing else to identify them, on a bench in the terminal waiting area at our gate. Now, coming and going from O'Hare Airport in Chicago all my life, I have experienced busy airports, but traffic in Heathrow shrinks that in an airport like O'Hare down to peanut size! I imagined those four little black-and-yellow rolls of film, like bees sitting in the crook of the bench, passed by thousands of travelers each moment.

Well, with unbending intent, my mother promptly wrote a letter to the lost and found department of Heathrow Airport upon our arrival in the States, determined to bring her precious recorders of time back home to us. By now you can guess what happened next. Yes, all four rolls returned safely at our doorstep, unharmed and in their original baggie. The timing was perfect too, as my great-grandmother passed away that February, and we were able to use the photos at her memorial services.

Mom's stories taught me a lot, namely that the universe has a plan for each of us and that which is meant to be mine cannot be taken from me. So now I pray often and I pray faithfully, knowing that every prayer is heard, and I always travel with Ganesh in my wallet.

Chapter 7

Priceless

Daily Affirmation #7:

"The universe supports me completely."

I remember getting the call while attending my first Abraham-Hicks' gathering: "Um, Seem, there's water coming up in your basement." It was my former husband, and he was with our kids at the house I inherited after the divorce. The mortgage-over-my-head house, left to me as a newly full-time single mom working overtime outside of the home, was now referred to as "my" house as the water came flooding in. The rains were torrential, but from the conference hall, there was little I could do about the situation except know it would all turn out all right. And that's exactly what I did—nothing.

Until I got home and saw the current reality: water up to the first stair of the basement and no relief in sight, as the city had just shut off the sewers due to citywide overflow. The only other place for the water to go was up through our homes. By morning, the water was approaching the second stair, and that's when it hit me that I was really on my own here. I sat down at the top of the stairs, put my head in my hands and cried. I could hear my children, four years old and just barely two, squealing and laughing upstairs. They didn't have a care in the world. I wanted a little piece of that. So I uttered a desperate prayer, and then I went up to play with them.

After a morning cup of tea, the phone rang. A friend had called to check in on us. When I described the situation with an air of hopeless letting go, she immediately sent her husband out for an electric water pump. In the state of emergency the entire city was in, finding a water pump in any store was no easy feat, but within a few hours, they had come to our rescue. After wading through the basement in fishing boots and hooking up all the equipment, my friend's husband had given us assurance that the pump was slowly sending the water from my basement out into the already flooded streets. We sat and watched. Just like the canals in Panama changing level, this was about as exciting as watching grass grow. In that quiet moment, I shared my gratitude for their help in turning around what had been defeat the night before. My friend's husband was aghast that I hadn't attempted more than a simple prayer, to which my friend quipped, "It sent you, didn't it?"

It turns out that the water pump was just the first of many answers to that one prayer, although each one showed up as a blessing in disguise. You see, it took four days for my basement to fill with over a foot of water from the sewers, and four more days for it to drain back out into the sewers. If only it had only taken just four more days to get damage control to come in for repairs. Instead, it took nearly four weeks, and by then, black mold had begun to grow about four feet up the walls. More concerning was the smell of basement that pervaded the house and mostly emanated from the baby's bedroom, which was all a mystery to me. Until the day I got another call I'll never forget, this one from the handyman who had just begun to assess the damage.

"Um, Seem, when you get back home, meet me in the driveway," he said.

I knew that couldn't be good. The baby and I had dropped off my preschooler at school and were coming from the library, just before I was headed off to work, but when I saw him emerge from my home with a gas mask in hand, my mind frantically searched for plan B, or plan C, or whatever plan was in play for that moment. Needless to say, we packed our bags and took up residence at a new location while demolition progressed. All the drywall came down (it wasn't so dry anymore, anyhow), all the support beams were treated and sprayed, and the bare guts of my foundation were exposed, revealing the most precious "gift" of all. On the southern wall of the basement, the previous tenant had hastily plastered a new piece of drywall atop an old piece of drywall, and that old piece had apparently molded many times over the years. Behind that old piece of drywall was the answer to the mysterious smell in the baby's room—an abandoned furnace vent with black mold growing up over two stories straight to the space over his crib. When I learned of their discovery, a fiery heat of anger flushed up my neck. How could my baby have been breathing mold for two years! And when that heat died down, I felt a cool wash of relief. Thank Goddess my baby breathed mold for *only* two years of his very long life. I blessed the flood that revealed a secret to better health.

The miracles hardly ended there. When my parents caught wind of our distress, they immediately contributed a brand new, energy-efficient washer and drier set, as the previous duo now had rusted-out parts. This new set could wash the clothes better and load twice as many as before, and for a single mom with little ones, this was its own miracle! Of course, we couldn't be sure yet of the condition of the boiler, a six thousand dollar top-of-the-line Weismann model from Germany we had installed as the first investment in upgrading the house. So when the serviceman removed the electrical plate and gasped, I nearly passed out.

"What did you find?" I queried with concern.

He rubbed his forehead and shook his head slightly as he replied, "You've got somebody looking out for you because the waterline comes just half an inch under the wires here. So I'm just going to clean it up a bit, and it should be good to go."

I finally breathed, and a big sigh of relief it was. Water four days filling, four days draining, four weeks sitting, and mold four feet up the walls . . . and four, of course, is a number of the angels, who were apparently swarming all around us.

The last piece of this story all happens behind the scenes, where most of what really matters in my stories happens. While I didn't lose sleep over financing the rebuilding of the basement, I did question often where the money might come from. That's when I received a call I might normally not have answered. It came from an automated voice, advising that our city had recently been declared a federal disaster area by FEMA and to check a certain web address for more information. We were all in such a rare state that something compelled me to investigate further. So, on a Friday after work, I stayed late to complete an application online. After forty-five arduous minutes and all but my blood type offered up to the government, my application had been submitted, and early on that Sunday morning, an inspector rang my front doorbell. After only a brief walk-through, he assured me that anything over one foot of water qualified for assistance and told me to expect some aid. What I didn't expect was for the government to deposit money into my account by Tuesday morning!

Now, the amount that came in covered half the repair costs, and I accepted it with gratitude. But it all gets better than that because on that Friday when the kids' dad came to pick them up, he came with an unexpected surprise in hand—our tax refund from the last year of filing jointly. And do you know the amount of the check? Yep, the other half of the repair costs!

Deconstruction and reconstruction: thousands of dollars. Brand new basement: zero dollars. Unmarked blessings in disguise: priceless.

Chapter 8

Born Ready

Daily Affirmation #8:

"I say 'yes' to life and it abundantly supplies me with all that I need."

I was fourteen years old, and it was the middle of winter in Chicago. After weeks of cold and cloudy weather, I rubbed the sleep out of my eyes one morning to wake up to the brightest shade of white I can recall, and I felt a little surge of enthusiasm course through me. The snow glistened and sparkled, like a new frontier. Not one footprint or bunny track anywhere to been seen, and it all happened overnight! Then, suddenly, the realization hit me. Could it be true? Too much snow for school?? This could mean only one thing: *snow day!*

Joy bubbled up inside me at the thought of the whole day ahead and nothing planned. After a customary bowl of cereal for breakfast, I layered on my thermal ware, clothes, and snow gear to head outside. I felt like a man on the moon exploring new turf, sinking into the fluff that came up well past my knees. After having my fill of snow angels, snowmen, and snowballs, a desire for something more welled up inside. The quiet of the day rang loudly with promise, and to me, it smelled like money! This opportunity to earn some cold cash by helping neighbors shovel themselves out called to me, and I set off with a shovel in hand.

I rang a few doorbells before becoming gainfully employed, and negotiations resulted in a twenty dollar exchange for a clear driveway (Okay, there really weren't any negotiations. I just said *"Pleeease?"* and my neighbor said, "How about twenty dollars?" At fourteen years old, that was a fortune to me!). Little did I know. You see, this was my first time actually working, and not playing, in the snow. I hadn't yet learned the little tricks like bending at the knees to use your leg muscles to lift, or how to push a trail through the snow to pattern a clearing path. On top of all that, I had unknowingly agreed to shovel a circle drive, which could have easily been the same surface area as three straight driveways! So I got straight to work. Scoop, lift, scoop, lift, scoop, lift, scoop.

About one hundred eight shovelfuls later, with an achy back and fatigue in my arms, I became aware of defeat creeping in. I took pause to assess the situation, and after brief calculations (I did become a math teacher after all), I realized that, yes, it would certainly take me a minimum of eight more hours to complete the job (Sigh.). But my determination to hold up my end of the contract was stronger than the doubt, and so I plowed along (pun very much intended here—keep reading!). I could hear a few birds waking up after the storm and the sound of my own breath panting to keep up with my body, and then there came a low rumble that grew increasingly louder and was coming my way. I looked up to see the plow guy clearing the streets.

Please allow me to digress for a moment. The village I grew up in had a population of three thousand when I was a girl. Now, I didn't grow up in a rural area; it was very much a part of modern suburbia. However, our section of the land was newly developing, and surrounded by other towns much more deeply established. When it came to municipalities, we had one town-hall room, four squad cars (which always felt like more than we needed to me), and, well, there's no "and." That's all we had. So this plow guy seemed to materialize out of nowhere that morning, and

I gazed longingly at the ease with which he moved through the snow in his big machine. Such power! Such speed! Such the *opposite* of what I had been huffing my way through!

He must have sensed it too, because my gaze poured right into his little cab, and he lifted a hand and waved at me. I waved back. And that little wave lifted my spirits enough for me to feel gratitude that I wasn't alone in this work. Contented, I truly thought that was the end of our little exchange until just as he passed by one end of the drive, he turned his mighty machine to enter the other end. *Has he slipped on the ice?* I wondered, until slowly, like creamy milk being poured into a tall glass of ice, it began to dawn on me that perhaps he had come to help! Sure as day, I suddenly realized that I stood in the direct path of that monster plow and leaped into the snowbank I had spent the last hour piling up. A yellow, buzzing blur powered past me, and somewhere inside all that I caught a glimpse of a smile. Then as quickly as he appeared from nowhere, he was gone again.

Who was that masked man? I heard in my head as I lay in the snow. I was stunned. Amazed! Basking in the warmth of the heavenly hand that had just been dealt to me. What a glorious sensation to go from the agony of defeat in the long day of labor ahead to the thrill of victory in the whole day ahead, with twenty dollars to boot!

That's when it occurred to me that I would need to cover up my tracks. Who would believe that a little girl like me could have plowed the whole drive in record time? Who would believe such a feat was humanly possible? I assessed the driveway and marked the few locations where evidence of a great plow revealed the secret to my superhuman powers. Using my little shovel, I broke up the plow-formed piles of snow into little chunks, putting my own bootprints atop their mounding masses. Satisfied that the driveway was clear and I had indeed addressed the entire perimeter, I sauntered back up to the front door.

My neighbor took his time answering the call, but finally arrived with wonder at my speedy return. Perhaps he thought my shovel had broken, or I'd been called to return home, or I needed a small favor before I could continue. Instead, he listened, and looked, in disbelief when I conveyed that the job was complete. As they say, "seeing is believing," and he could see that the driveway was clear. And so our contract was honored and I walked home with my cash in hand.

I had never heard of the Law of Attraction when I was fourteen, but it's clear to me that not knowing about it doesn't mean it isn't real. Not knowing about the force of gravity doesn't mean that it won't apply to you. In childhood, our desires are pure, our beliefs are mainly aligned with our Source, and even among the most difficult of circumstances, we are likely to notice the experience of grace. That snowy morning beamed with extraordinary promise unlike most days, and I am grateful that I chose to say "yes," trusting in the wonder of all the day would bring.

Chapter 9

Chubby Little Mouse

Daily Affirmation #9:

"All that I desire flows to me easily."

I often imagine a world where children never forget their power to create their own reality, and I make my best effort to impart what I remember to my own children. So I never tire of telling this next tale, which I credit fully to my daughter's creative powers, since it brings me to a state of awe and gratitude for the wonderful teacher to me that she was born to be.

During a stroll through the mall one morning, searching for an indoor-weather diversion on a cloudy winter day, my daughter and I passed a toy shop with a whizzing mechanical ferret chasing a ball in the window. The lure drew us in, hook, line, and sinker. Up and down the aisles of toys we floated, her searching for the grandest (read: most expensive) treasure she could acquire, and me searching for the rarest little gem (read: under five dollars) to suit her needs.

Suddenly, her eyes lit up with glee. "I want *this* one, Mommy!" she squealed, handing me a set with a pocket-sized Cinderella and her various accessories. My brows furrowed quizzically as I wondered if she had the very same little doll already at home. But this clever little girl caught on quickly, stumbling for a good reason to have *this* one instead. I watched her intently, almost too much so, as her pudgy little toddler finger careened over the chubby little figurine of Gus, Cinderella's tiny mouse friend.

"Is it that you really want this mouse, honey?" I probed as her shy grin told the whole truth. Gently, I broke it to her—okay, maybe not so gently—that in no way would I be spending that amount of money to bring home a tiny one-inch mouse from a set that contained the precise toys she currently kept at home. However, I reminded her in the very next breath of her own creative powers to receive everything she has ever wanted, even if I could not currently serve as her channel to receive these things. Enough said.

A few days passed by, and our regular routine carried on. Library reading group on Monday, Mom-and-tot gymnastics on Tuesday, playgroup on Wednesday, and then a magically ordinary playdate at our neighbor's home. Since her birth, my daughter had played at my neighbor's home, daily for the first year while I went to work and then weekly thereafter. She had mapped out every square inch of the home, noting the location where each of her favorite toys were stashed away as well as the location where the toys designed to distract the babies from her favorite toys were strategically positioned. Darting from one spot to the next, she greeted the toys one by one and merrily tended to them all. My neighbor and I had quickly become engrossed in our coffees and conversation when my daughter darted toward me, cheering, "Mommy, look what I found!" Panting with excitement, she lay in the palm of my hand one chubby little mouse, and not just any mouse, and not just a one-inch mouse, but a peach-portioned chubby *great* mouse figurine of Gus. We had played in that house hundreds of times before, and yet on this day, Gus seemed to materialize from out of nowhere. I smiled. I knew she would discover all that she ever wanted, and it seemed in this moment she knew it too.

The story seems complete here, but just as I thought that, her friend came bouncing over to declare, "You can have that, if you want it." The deal was sealed. That was it. My baby girl had been officially declared a Magnificent Creator!

Chapter 10

Lights, Camera, Action!

Daily Affirmation #10:

"I use my mind and my thoughts to create a life I love."

Thoughts are very real things. Oh, if I only knew then what I know now!

I thought the pediatric nurse was nuts when she thought that I was suicidal, but something in my face gave away my misery. Her concern gave me pause (Thank heavens!). What did she see that I was blind to? Pushing a newborn in a stroller with a toddler in tow, I took myself for the average overworked mom. I thought it was normal for a mother to feel like a zombie when caring for two children under the age of two, and maybe it is, but that doesn't mean it was right. With my then-husband golfing through his "paternity" leave and working overtime upon his return to the office, I continued to chant the mantra, "I'm a single mom," beating the drum of my unwanted existence right into reality.

Some days the pain of my loneliness felt so unbearable. Of course, the familiarity of the pain sat with me like an old friend, one I had known since childhood, growing up in a home with excessive conflict. I had become pretty adept at escaping to the only safe place I could find: my mind. I could create fantasies like no other! I had swum deep oceans as a mermaid, floated past undiscovered planets in space, and fed unicorns in fields of wildflowers at the end of the rainbow. As I matured, however, so did the nature of my fantasies.

Perhaps I should have noticed a red flag when I began to schedule my university courses around my favorite soap opera. With so many years of draaaaaaah-ma being ingested through my eyes, I might have expected it to show up in my own life, but it all took me completely by surprise.

For so many days and nights I would rock back and forth nursing my baby, each of us lulling the other into a state so peaceful that a smooth exit from my daily toils opened up so easily every time. Off my mind would go to the nearest target: the tall, dark, and handsome "other" man. My mind concocted dreamy dialogues, the gentleness of a large hand on my low back, the warmth of soft breath on my neck, the sense of urgency in feelings unspoken for years. The scenes in my mind played out as though straight from the movie screens that have lured countless viewers for over a century to a classic fantasy of rescue-me-from-doldrums. It brought me relief, and it seemed harmless enough, until one misty early spring morning.

The smell of rain lingered in the air. My flannel pajamas kept me cozy and warm as our usual morning breakfast routine unfolded; and like many growing and changing infants, my baby's napping pattern created a sense of mystery about how each day might unfold. On this morning, however, something mystical lingered in the air, and just after nine o'clock, my baby let out one big yawn. Without batting an eyelash, all three of us headed upstairs. My toddler went to play with some toys—quietly and independently, for the first time in my memory—and my baby laid down to rest without so much as a peep. Before I could even shut the bedroom door, my cell phone began to ring.

Now, this was the first unusual event, because those who know me, know I waded slowly and cautiously into the technical age. So at the time, this was an emergency-use-only kind of device. The second unusual event was the identity of the caller, who from here on out I shall simply refer to as the "other man." And the third unusual event was his pronouncement that he stood outside my front door. Amazed at all the comings together—my toddler contentedly occupied and my baby sleeping upstairs—I opened the door.

What unfolded next was a scene I had seen played out over and over again in my mind, in full living color.

For a moment after I shut the door behind him, I stood in wonder at what had just happened. My fantasy—now a reality? It was as though I were a movie director, and he an actor in a scene scripted in detail and executed masterfully. Could it be that *I* was the creator of this drama? Could it be that *I* had so much power to align the planets just so to realize my every desire?

When I called my dearest girlfriend in a mortified awe, she calmly acknowledged that I had been working on this for quite some time. I had garnered quite a lot of momentum behind this fantasy during the decade this man and I had been friends. The story was truly quite unoriginal, but that I had lived it from my own flesh-and-blood existence amazed me so! And as my friend bore witness to the unfolding events, I received the greatest, and most frightening, gift of all: knowing that indeed *I had done this.*

Now, admittedly, this was not the proudest moment of my life. I mistook my daydreams as innocuous musings. But as it turns out, thoughts are very real things, and if we stay with them long enough, we will even find that they show up in what we call our reality. Imagine the implications of that! So much focused effort, so much emotion, so much wanting, so much desire, and so much *power* to orchestrate time and space to make it come about. If I could do *that*, what could I do next?

The thought nearly paralyzed me. You know what they say, "Be careful what you wish for."

Chapter 11

My Angels of Information

Daily Affirmation #11:

"I move through life and know that I am safe—
Divinely protected and guided."
—Louise Hay, *I Can Do It!*

*M*y whole life changed course on a Monday night.
I'll always remember it was a Monday night because I had just finished a phone call with my closest girlfriend, one in which I expressed my desire to terminate my budding emotional affair through disclosure. She responded with caution, pleading with me to wait. She argued that talking to my then husband about it on Friday would afford us both the chance to let the news settle in over the weekend, and we could recover in time for work again the following Monday. At the time, her advice seemed absurd to me. "I don't want to live this way for another day, let alone another week," I told her, and I impetuously awaited his exit from the shower.

It had been months since I'd attempted any conversation of real depth with him. Our marriage had been a boiling pot of unresolved childhood hurts and traumas, and on this Monday, it came to a head. Our babies slumbered peacefully in their cribs, and the chorus of crickets droned outside. An eerie stillness hovered over our home. Then I dropped the bomb.

Once he allowed the meaning of my message to sink in, he naturally exploded. He puffed his chest like a peacock. The veins in his thick neck bulged under his skin. His eyes filled with a dark red rage. And I took shelter, pulling myself into a little ball on the couch, waiting for the storm to pass. When it did, the air cleared and a wave of calm rolled in.

He exhaled. Then he dropped *his* bomb. "This is karma, you know. I've been expecting this for quite some time." He had gotten hooked into some online habits, and his intention in sharing with me was to alleviate any guilty feelings over my own transgressions. Some people might say this was an "opportunity" to bring about healing and a deeper level of intimacy within a relationship. But for me, this news was a deal-breaker. I was in shock, feeling betrayed, mirroring his emotions over my admission. I had been in denial for nearly a decade, not wanting to know the underlying issues creating cracks in the foundation of our eroding marriage. But in this moment, it was undeniable.

Then the sudden recall of a memory graced me, and changed me forever.

Just one week before that fateful Monday night, the two of us engaged in our routine nighttime activities. He was watching his favorite shows on TV, and I was surfing the web. Then, from seemingly nowhere, an alert appeared to warn me against proceeding to the next page. It never appeared before, nor ever since. I had to read the warning a few times before it made any sense to me, and when it finally registered, I showed it to him, hoping he could explain such an electronic mystery. Perturbed at the interruption of his show and piqued by the content of the warning, he looked at it, he paused, and then he answered flatly, "I don't know."

And I believed him. You see, my computer and his computer were both housed in our home office, but on their own desks, in their own corners of the room. I never used his, and he never used mine. So what could be the explanation for this electronic communication?

I may never have a definite answer to that question, but I choose to believe this: I am surrounded by spirits who seek modes of communication in ways I can hear. Apparently, my angels wanted to prepare me for what was to unfold that night, perhaps to lessen the aftershock. I am also clear that the decade of my lack of knowledge served us all well, for in my ignorance, I was able to usher our two children into a beautiful and loving world, and they now benefit from the joys of two housefuls of love. I rest assured every day that in every moment, I know everything I need to know, and that I am always divinely protected.

Chapter 12

An Impeccable Solution

Daily Affirmation #12:

"There is a solution to every problem."
—Louise Hay, *Heart Thoughts*

"*A*re we there yet?"

I have not only asked this question from the back seat of my parents' car as a kid, but also as an adult on my way to manifesting the next new cocreation with Life. Yet, I know from years in my kitchen that some recipes require slow simmering to blend flavors together to perfection, and from years in my garden that tending to small seeds sown can reap harvests during the right season. Still, I found myself asking this question nearly every day when it became evident that my marriage was approaching its end.

We had been in therapy for months, attempting "to squeeze orange juice from lemons," as one of my friends called it. Weariness began settling in as our conversations grew shorter and the inevitable approached. I remember the sunny afternoon, after the last guest had left a small gathering at our home, when I sat at the dining table exhausted. He shut the door and exclaimed, "Do you want a divorce, or what?" His question still lingered in the air like a cartoon bubble when I heard my own voice reply *"Yes"* without hesitation. Then came the pause. Silence. It's like Billy Crystal says in *When Harry Met Sally*: it was already out there, and now I couldn't take it back.

Nor did I want to. I had meant it, and the universe had heard me.

The next morning, I awoke in a sleepy haze. During those days, I sometimes had difficulty distinguishing between events that happened in my sleep state and my waking state. Both seemed equally "real" to me, for the first time that I can remember. So to see my mother-in-law sitting in my kitchen so early on a Sunday morning made me question my whereabouts. The last day of my summer break from teaching had arrived, and something serious hung heavily in the air. Had she heard our conversation the day before from miles away? Had she sensed the doom that knocked on our door? Had she come in one last attempt to revive a marriage from its deathbed?

In fact, the answer to all of the above was "no." She had come on her own personal mission, her own parallel mission, to let us know that she needed us to find a new sitter for our babies that year. She was leaving her husband. She had rented an apartment, on the doctor's orders, when her breathing became labored in her home due to her husband's hoarding. Oddly enough, it turned out that the apartment right next door to her home was available for rent. While to most, this would seem not quite far enough away, to her, it was the perfect distance. As she explained it, this allowed her to still cook for her husband (She is a natural born caretaker!) and also have space of her own. However, the two bedrooms provided more space than she actually needed, and she couldn't afford the apartment on her own. So she wanted to find a full-time job to support herself. Watching her grandchildren while we worked had become a luxury she couldn't afford anymore.

My heart sunk. My stomach lurched. With so much on my plate already, I could hardly understand how to make this all work, and on such tight timing—overnight, it would seem, since work began again the next day! Thankfully, she promised to stay with our babies until we could all find a suitable solution. She departed with a heavy heart after delivering her message, and no sooner did the door shut when I felt a wave of glee come over me. "This is it!" I exclaimed in joy as he furrowed his brows at me with disapproving surprise and frustration. Had I gone insane? Our world had crumbled before us, and I was squealing with delight? How could I find happiness in all that had unfolded during the last twenty-four hours? But it was a powerful moment because I had been graced with an insight that all we had been asking for had just aligned perfectly!

"This is it!" I explained. "Your mom has an extra bedroom, and now you have a place to go!" I smiled. I had prayed. The universe had answered me, and it had answered overnight.

I recall feeling such a deep satisfaction that morning knowing that inherent in every problem lies its own perfect solution. What a perfect plan the universe offers us! I mean, every lock is sold with its own key. We wouldn't imagine it any other way. So why would the universe offer us any problem without its own solution? We can access it every time, without fail, if we simply open up to receiving it. The solution may not come in the form we expect, but that could be because we only see it from our own personal perspective. When the divinely inspired solution arrives, I find that it typically serves all the parties involved.

Now, he didn't quite see it all the same way, but it turned out that he eventually did move in to that apartment, which helped his mother pay the rent. This allowed her to continue spending her days with her grandchildren (which she lovingly deems "the greatest joy of her life") while we went to work. He got a fresh start with the support of his family and familiar neighbors surrounding him. And best of all, when our kids visited their dad's new apartment, they ate home-cooked meals brought from next door by their grandmother and shared time playing with their grandfather. As for me, I finally found an inner freedom I hadn't felt in years, and everyone prospered.

Chapter 13

Where There's a Will

Daily Affirmation #13:

"Life loves me!"
—Louise Hay

Sometimes the desire for something to happen is so great that it doesn't really matter much if you believe it will. It just does.

So it was with my first boyfriend. After years of being a third wheel to my best friend and her boyfriend at the time, I had conjured up a lot of ideas about how wonderful the coming of *my* first love affair would be. As a Pisces, fantasy comes easily to me, but the meeting of my first love pushed the limits of my little mind's imagination! Spring break, my senior year in high school, and a class outing to Hawaii drew a crew of twelve of us girls. Having received acceptance papers to the colleges of our choices, we packed our bags with flip-flops, sundresses, and bikinis and set off for Waikiki Beach. Our arrival was as subtle as a flashing neon bar sign, and soon young men began to flock all around us. Before long, my roommates had each paired up with a military man, but not me. I had my vision, and I stubbornly stuck to it. Nothing less would do. Nothing less felt good enough. Until one evening . . .

The boys had dragged another holdout back at the barracks to come out with us. I noticed him hanging back most of the evening, quiet. It got me wondering about his story, and when a private opportunity on the lanai presented itself, I seized the moment to ask. Some hours later, we were strolling hand in hand along the shoreline, floating in time, absorbed in being, delighted to have such interest in each other's offerings. Perched in a lifeguard tower, we witnessed the most magnificent spectacle of falling stars I have ever seen, before or since. I don't recall watching the sun rise early that morning, but I do vividly remember the ecstasy of passing a magical week in paradise together.

Soon the time to depart descended upon us. The scene played out like one from a war movie: a charter bus with luggage being loaded aboard, and boys with buzz cuts unable to release from the embrace of their girls, who were unable to stop their tears from flowing. It seemed almost comical, even then. The truth was, we hardly knew each other. We just knew it felt good to be together, and we wanted more of that. So we exchanged addresses and bid adieu. Hoping for a next time. Praying for a next time.

Months passed, and summer approached. College days beckoned us, and the next chapter of life would begin. Almost desperate to keep the connection alive, one of the boys came to visit my girlfriend in Chicago. It seemed to me this visit would solidify what they had started. It would turn fly-by-night romantics into a devoted couple. (Again, a Piscean fantasy-maker, remember?) How I envied her so deeply! How I ached to relive just a moment of what we had created on that tropical isle! How easily it seemed to happen for her.

When I had the chance to talk with my soldier in Hawaii, I know he could hear the despair and longing in my voice. I could hear it in his as well. But his mom expected him home for leave that year, and our next meeting would have to be shelved for the time being. We vowed we would wait for each other, but honestly, I wasn't sure we could. Life happens. Things change. College would be starting soon, and I didn't know what would come next. All I wanted was one more meeting. One more chance just to see his face. I was certain this would tell me if my heart could, or would want to, go on with our long-distance affair.

I suppose I surrendered any notion of control shortly thereafter, for it is said that things happen when we least expect them to. That's when I got the call from him. His voice had changed. The energy had shifted. "Seem," he said in his Southern drawl, "they had to reroute my flight home this summer, and guess where the layover is now . . . Chicago!"

Boo-ya! It was a miracle! I once heard "miracle" defined as "manifestation of the wanted," and this certainly qualified as wanted. Well, kinda. While I hoped for more, it seemed the universe had heard my request quite literally and aligned everything so I could have "one more chance to just see his face" again. The divinely scripted details of our meeting permitted half an hour amidst his transit. And just writing this makes me smile with the knowing of how much Life loves me, since that half an hour fell precisely on the afternoon my father had already asked me to drive him to the airport for a flight out that same day! A miracle? I'd say so.

More amazing than our first two meetings were all our subsequent meetings. One after another we managed, through our hearts' strong desire, to enjoy visiting each other, stretching for weeks at a time, several times a year. Eventually, we did split up and go our own ways, when the time came to move on. But I often reminisced about how we seemed to yield the power that creates worlds to bring ours together. And then we did it again.

As I graduated college and prepared to move on to the next chapter of my life, I wondered what it might be like to spend one more evening with him. Back then I think I called it "finding closure." By this time, however, he had moved away, and this was well before the popularity of the World Wide Web or even before the inception of Facebook (Can you imagine such an era?). So how we reconnected exactly, I can't say, but I can say I wasn't the least bit surprised to learn he had recently moved to the same town in Florida where I would be departing for a cruise vacation, with the same girlfriend I spent my spring break with in Hawaii. That allowed us one night, one last night to wrap it up, to tie a bow on our time together, to say goodbye.

Sometimes when I share with others that our thoughts and words create our own realities, they wonder why their dictated realities don't manifest. They'll exclaim something cheeky like, "I want to win the lottery!" just to offer me evidence against the Law of Attraction when they don't win it. This method cleverly challenged me to investigate the potent ingredient that allows the formula to function. In the case of the relationship with this military man, my experiences delivered every time. I asked, and I received, every time. The universe never denies us. Only we can deny ourselves, with our disbelief in what we ask for (Did they *really* expect to win the lottery?). So what was the missing ingredient that revealed one miracle after another during the years of this relationship? One word: emotion. My belief that our relationship could not be sustained over the years of distance between us eventually dominated, but there was no parallel for the power of emotion that set the energy in motion during those wonderful years we cocreated together. For me, the experience of a first love conjured up the deep emotion necessary for the Law of Attraction to yield to my desires, but I'm certain you can think of many more examples.

Chapter 14

The License Plate Game

Daily Affirmation #14:

"My thoughts are focused and clear."

The word "DETOXX" was scribed in capital yellow letters against a navy background on the license plate in front of me. How fitting, since I was driving to my weekly therapy appointment, thinking about how to move past the drama that had exploded in my marriage that year, and really feeling the need to shed the toxic buildup of words and deeds gone awry. My own thoughts were reflected back to me so glaringly in that vanity plate that I took a closer look and noticed the origin of the plate: Alaska. To quote my youngest, "You don't see that every day!" Especially not in Chicago, or perhaps anywhere in the mainland USA. Certainly it was a rare sight, but even rarer was the fact that the aforementioned "other man" had once boasted to me of his most unique unseen trait: having been born in Alaska. Just in case I'd missed the signs before, this plate was one clear message that it was time to cleanse and detoxify from thoughts that had not served my highest good.

The encounter with that plate sparked a new found interest in fine-tuning my attraction powers. For nearly a decade driving around

Illinois, the only outside license plates I ever noticed were from North Carolina, "First in Flight." Simplemindedly, I wondered why so many people from North Carolina would be visiting Illinois while people from other states rarely seemed to come around, even those from bordering states like Indiana, Michigan, or Wisconsin. Why North Carolina? Not that I minded. Every time I saw a NC plate, I slipped into a dreamy virtual reality of living on the beach with my first love, the military man. Until one day it occurred to me that the one common denominator in all these chance happenings was me. Could it be that perhaps I had been dreamily drifting off to a Carolina coast *before* the plate passed by, thus drawing the sight of that plate to me? In hindsight, I had some level of awareness of the Law of Attraction long before I studied it more formally, as we are all keenly aware of gravity long before a physics professor ever details its properties to us. But after I learned about the law, the license plates became a playful challenge. I was ready to flex my attraction powers and test myself with the plates: Alabama, Alaska, Arizona, Arkansas, California, Colorado . . . I wanted to see them *all*! And not while visiting all fifty states, but here in my hometown. I wanted to prove to myself that I had let the past go, that I had shifted my vibration from a pattern that repetitively showed me the same outcome every time, that I had control over the signal I was sending out, attracting whatever I chose to focus on, and that doing so could be as simple as I allowed it to be. Abraham's words, "It is as easy to create a castle as a button," rang in my ears. I was ready. Let the games begin!

My vision broadened quickly. Ah, of course! Neighboring states' plates poured into my line of sight. One by one, Iowa, Kentucky, Ohio, even Nebraska, Pennsylvania, and the Dakotas, leapt out at me, competing for a top spot in the race to the finish line. Expecting to see the larger contenders like California, Texas, and New York, I honed in on the underdogs like Rhode Island, Maine, and Delaware. Not that I kept a list or anything, checking it twice, as Santa Claus would, but I could feel when I'd get a "hit," or when I would spy a rare gem or a private message like "DETOXX" sent just for me from the universe. During the months, and years, that my grown-up version of the license plate game carried on, I became privy to plates I never knew existed, like the 2007 series of the Consular and Diplomatic Corp. I suppose living in a more ethnically diverse neighborhood could have contributed to the likelihood of such plates. But I still can't account for the plate which came from no state at all; it had a "4" on it and it read, "Supreme Court." The best I can figure is that it was my personal invitation to carry on with the game.

It became clear that something within me had shifted and that I was releasing old patterns. I felt exhilarated pointing out the rarest of plates to my unsuspecting, captive passengers who looked on with wonder and amazement, whether because the plate appeared or because I delighted so much in it showing up. Heavy traffic became lighthearted fun, and more and more I began to feel in control of at least one thing in my crazy life: focus.

Then one day, it hit me. I could see the end of the road, the checkered flag, the finish line of the game between me, myself, and I, and it looked like a rainbow. A Hawaiian rainbow, to be specific. That would be my mark of mastery, mastering the art of focusing energy with such precision and attunement that I could metaphorically create a castle (or a button!). And so I set out expecting, happily anticipating, the sighting of a Hawaiian license plate in Chicago.

At first I scoured the streets, north and south, east and west, like a hawk hunting prey. The intensity of my desire scared even me a bit, until eventually I learned to relax. Then the moment came. July 19, 2011, pulling out of a movie-theater parking lot after an afternoon matinee with the kids. In the mess of validating the parking tickets and lining up at the shortest of the four pay stalls, I pulled up right behind that car just as the traffic light turned red. Blessed little red light, forcing me to pause in all our clamoring to exit the garage and just notice, notice we had pulled up behind a Hawaiian license plate. Aloha! Victory was mine! Mission accomplished. The game was complete. Until it went on.

That fall, just a few months later, I saw a second Hawaiian license plate on the car in front of our minivan as it pulled out of my children's elementary school after dismissal. Shock? Disbelief. Elation! I felt invincible, really. I had done it again. But perhaps you've sensed by now that three is my magic number, and as I mentioned before, it's on the third time around that I have definite confirmation from my Source that I'm on target.

As I sifted through my evidence, searching for the most impactful seventeen stories to share with you, the ones that lend the most credence to the power of the Law of Attraction, I had doubts about how veritable this child's game of "I Spy" could be. Although there's a certain logic in sharing a story about license plates when it was my very own license plate that spurred this investigative inquiry, I posed the question of whether to write this chapter or not soon after the new year began. Then, leaving my friend's home in the city during the Super Bowl game, I spied the very reason you're reading this chapter now: the third Hawaiian plate, blanketed in snow.

Chapter 15

My Body Knows

Daily Affirmation #15:

"I listen with love to my body's messages."
—Louise Hay, *Life! Reflections on Your Journey*

"Mom, can I wait to go to the ER until morning, or do you think I'll die tonight?"

Crazier than my having asked this question was my mom's response: "Go to bed, honey. The ER is insane in the middle of the night! Get some rest, and then go in the morning, around seven or eight before it gets too busy again for the day."

Mom has been a practicing physician for over forty years, but the fact I called her for advice signaled to me how dire my situation was. After all, mom is a psychiatrist, and severe edema is not her specialty.

Edema, as defined on Wikipedia's website, is "an abnormal accumulation of fluid in the interstitium, which are locations beneath the skin or in one or more cavities of the body." From my hip down to my pinky toe, my entire right leg had swollen so badly that when I pressed my thumb into the skin, the pitting remained for minutes thereafter. This happens sometimes to pregnant women, and I too had seen it during my first pregnancy when I was still teaching five classes a day, on my feet all the time, and waddling around the halls wearing thirty plus pounds more than I had ever carried on my body in my life. I suppose the swelling under those conditions was to be expected. But at this point, I was the healthiest I had ever felt. I had been gradually changing my thoughts and gradually shifting the course of my life. I was practicing yoga daily and teaching it twice a week. And it was just days before during practice that I had noticed for the first time how taxed my internal systems had become. I labored for breath holding my first downward-facing dog, feeling my heart pounding so fiercely I feared the others practicing would hear it beating. Every organ had maxed out its capacity to the degree there was little energy left for my muscles or my mind. So what had caused all of this?

Three weeks prior, I had noticed a small pimple-like bump on my right shin, which at first I suspected to be an ingrown hair, like those I occasionally get after waxing my legs. So I kept watch over it, even using hot compresses in an attempt to open the pore, and when a little crater appeared there after a week, I knew this was not the garden-variety ingrown hair. In fact, nothing could possibly stand a chance of growing there, as the yellow pus that oozed from this spot indicated a legitimate infection. My sincerest apologies for having gotten so graphic about it, but I want to stress how obviously wrong things seemed to be going before I awoke to the clear signal that the time had come for me to take action.

You see, I fully believe that the body possesses an innate intelligence to heal naturally. Living with not one, but two, physicians as a child, I witnessed the effects, and non-effects, of Western medicine on the body. The little pills worked for me when I needed them to, and they often accelerated the process my body would have naturally taken. So when I finally experienced that the same healing could effectively take place without the side effects of Western medicines, I began to allow my body the time to heal on its own. My body *does* know how to heal naturally, and it knows how to communicate to me with clear, strong signals, and the pus coming from my shin was an obvious white flag of distress. It needed reinforcements, and fast!

A visit to the school nurse affirmed what I didn't want to hear. "You need antibiotics, Seema!" she exclaimed, amazed this little pimple had formed into a volcanic crater so quickly. That's when I heard my little ego voice smugly claim a small victory, as I was already taking an antibiotic, three times a day: oil of oregano.

Rewind with me a few more months, if you will. Through referrals of trusted colleagues, I visited a holistic dermatologist who practices under the premise that the skin is an external reflection of the internal state of the body. She traced the roots of my skin condition to excess candida in the gut and ordered me on a strict diet to flush out the toxins before delivering any dermatological treatments. The diet consisted of eliminating all sugars and yeast and adding in apple cider vinegar, probiotics, and carefully monitored doses of oil of oregano, a natural, and potent, antibiotic.

My ego voice continued to monopolize the conversation between me and my body for another two weeks, offering well-intentioned but very damaging reassurance that everything was covered and the natural antibiotic I supplied my body with would suffice. My edema finally interrupted.

The pain was so severe I couldn't even walk up the stairs. That's when I pulled out my laptop to do a little bit more Internet investigation. I scanned through medical sites probing for any information that resembled the caldera on my leg, and then it appeared: abscess. Next, I searched for what Louise Hay might say about an abscess, and while I didn't find her interpretation on the Internet (you'll have to read it in her book *You Can Heal Your Body*), I did find another gem from her website which you can read about in the next chapter. So I'll leave it to you, the reader, to research the details of abscesses further, if you care to, but suffice it to say that I knew enough now to rest comfortably and drive myself to the ER in the morning, if I didn't die overnight.

Mom was right, I must admit, that 7 a.m. seemed to be the quietest and simplest time for an ER visit. The doctor barely blinked at my leg before he prepared his tools. After a minor incision and some painful swabbing, he invited me to rest comfortably while he ran some tests on the sample. The nurse and I chatted about everyday affairs for a while, and after a natural lull in our dialogue, I mentioned the only insurmountable illness I could recall having before, strep throat. It struck me as a child, and that may not be significant as a stand-alone fact, but I found the timing to be remarkable. It affected me during the same year my mother was working full time as a doctor and overtime as a student, spending weeks on end in the hospital without coming home. I recall having visits with her by the hospital vending machine during short respites between patient calls. My heart ached for her, and I longed to have her tuck me in bed at night and cuddle me close. I kept the pain of it inside, because I could see how hard she was working too, and I wanted everything to work out for her, but inside, I was screaming for attention. The screams must have gotten stuck there, and when my throat swelled shut, they couldn't ignore me anymore. I suppose the memories dwelled in my mind because they had become the main target for processing during current sessions with my psychotherapist. Now here I lay in a hospital bed once again, some thirty years later, sick again.

I couldn't have been better prepared, then, for what the doctor revealed when he returned with the lab results.

"It appears that you have a streptococcus bacterial infection of the skin," he declared.

I was momentarily stunned. "Are you telling me, Doctor, that my leg has strep throat?"

Maybe he had never heard it stated quite that way before, but it was clear to me that's what it was! He called in a prescription of antibiotics to my local drugstore, and I succumbed to the aid of Western medicines, praising my body for the great work it had done in the past three weeks on such a tough little bacteria and assuring it I would step in with reinforcements. I took the antibiotics with mixed emotions of gratitude for the immediate relief all of my internal systems experienced, and reluctance due to a lingering memory of the fungal infections that would always follow, but the most amazing part about my experience with the antibiotics this time was the absence of any side effects at all! Could it have been a result of the candida cleanse? Could it have been aligning my beliefs with the right action at the right time? I may not have direct assurance of the reason to offer, but I do believe that little (and big) miracles happen every day.

That could be the end of this story, and I'm so grateful that it's not! You see, I have a whole staff of alternative healers in my virtual rolodex, and on this occasion, I decided to schedule a tune-up with my acupuncturist just for good measure. Upon relaying the same story to her that I've shared with you now, she smiled approvingly. She confirmed that to treat my aforementioned symptoms, she would needle the *shu* point for the digestive tract, which would fall at precisely the same location as the abscess on my shin, and now it seemed that would be unnecessary since my body had already made a natural opening for a release from that same location. Then she commended me, and my body, for having worked the illness all the way down from my throat through my digestive tract, and out the bottom of my being back into the earth to be recycled.

In the years that have followed since that day, I loving smile at the scar that remains on my leg—a lasting reminder of the true genius of the body.

Chapter 16

To Get a New Dream

Daily Affirmation #16:

"I Can Do It!"
—Louise Hay, *I Can Do It!*

When I introduced myself to the gal sitting next to me in the shuttle van, she smiled at me with familiarity. She had flown on the same plane to Tucson as I had, and she had overheard my conversation about flying to the Miraval Resort for a conference. She carried on to say she felt relieved to know that someone else (me!) knew where she was headed, and that she'd simply follow me from the baggage claim to find her way. This was the first time I had breathed all day, maybe even for weeks. For goodness sake, I was sitting in the Miraval shuttle van, and I still had doubts if I was in the right place!

The story goes way back. After spending decades in school, at first learning and then teaching, I had become adept at planning and creating marvelous spring breaks. The one in Italy was just the beginning. The next year, a dozen of us sorority gals sunned the days away in Cancun, and each year thereafter I have planned a trip to rejuvenate and revive after a long winter. This year was no different. I had searched fervently for the perfect trip, and to say that what came about surpassed my expectations would be an understatement.

When I began reading and studying Abraham-Hicks's teachings years ago, I immersed myself in their lectures, recordings, and website. Like a sponge, I soaked up as much as I could, feeling quite alive. One evening online, I noticed that they offered a Caribbean cruise with daily lectures aboard a marvelous ship among some of the most joy-filled folks around. Better than all that, it was during the exact same dates as my spring break! The only problem was that it also happened to be the same year I was divorcing. That might have been the first time I put a kibosh on my travel plans (Although looking back, that cruise was a perfect invitation for positive transformation!). I then vowed that the next time the stars aligned to offer me this excursion, nothing would stop me from jumping at the chance. So years later, I really felt as though my time to cruise with Abraham-Hicks had finally come, but alas, not only did the cruise dates not correspond to my spring break, they weren't even cruising in the spring! Strike one.

Now, for some years I had also asked my yoga teacher to plan a "field trip" to Thailand for our studio. She spends three weeks there every August studying with her teacher and returns home to the studio radiant and renewed, with the smell of coconut wafting behind her. I wanted a taste of that, and I wanted to do it alongside her. To have our teacher to show us the ropes of a new country and deepen our practice in a paradise setting. Finally, that too came together, and I was beyond thrilled! The only problem was that the dates didn't correspond to my spring break. Nor did it make sense, as I knew her kids' school was on break the same week our school was on break. But it was out of our hands, since the studio in Thailand couldn't accommodate us that week. Strike two.

Public school teachers do have a generous vacation allotment, this is true. It is also true that when travel is concerned, each travel segment is a high-demand peak period. They always take place during the time when non-teaching parents take their kids somewhere fantastic, and ticket availability thus decreases. So did my motivation for finding the right getaway. I spent much of that winter battling the abscess on my shin, a painful, can't-walk-up-the-stairs kind of an abscess. As I sat at my breakfast bar, limp from the pain, I wondered what Louise Hay would have said about an abscess. Her little book *You Can Heal Your Body* sat at my bed stand. It had become a sort of Diagnostic and Statistical Manual for me—the diagnostic tool I used for every malady, big or small just as psychiatrists use the DSM in their practices. Just the thought of walking upstairs made my shin throb, so I hopped online to see if her "list" might be there. Of course, it was not (You'll have to buy the book if you want to know what it says about an abscess, or any other dis-ease, and I highly recommend that you do!), but what I found instead was a miracle. An awesome, amazing, God-sitting-at-the-breakfast-bar-with-me kind of a miracle.

When I first started planning spring breaks as a single traveler after my divorce, I allowed myself to be treated to places I might never have thought I deserved before. Oprah's list seemed like a good place to start, and in one of her magazines was a list of her top five favorite resort spas. As you've probably already guessed, Miraval was on that list, but that's not where I'm going with this. I'd seen her show on Miraval already. I knew how five-star and out-of-my-league it was, or so I thought. No, I settled on something more intriguing, and more local: The Raj in Iowa. I figured that by driving there, I could divert the money saved on airfare to help pay for my stay without giving up my firstborn child. It was the most I'd splurged on a vacation ever, and it was a once in a lifetime kind of a splurge, or so I thought.

But back to Louise's site. Not finding the list, I found something even better: a conference held by Louise herself at Miraval exactly during the dates of my spring break. Could it really be? Abraham-Hicks Cruise—strike one. Yoga in Thailand—strike two. Louise at Miraval—home run? I checked my school calendar to be sure. I checked her site again to be double sure. I checked my school calendar at least a dozen times between that night and the next. Home run! Yes, this was the one thing I had dreamed of every moment of every day, and here it was in front of me. I had invited Louise countless times to the dinner party in my head, the one where you can invite any five people, dead or alive. You've played this one too, right? Or maybe it's just me. The list kept revolving, but Louise's spot at my dinner table was always secure. And this was my chance to learn directly from her. Nothing could stop me now, except the price.

You have to know that when the price listed is "call for pricing," you can't afford it if you have to ask. So I took a deep breath. I closed my eyes. And I had a calm conversation with my self. What would the price have to be to say "no"? Here is a woman whose eighty-four years of life's work had changed my whole way of being. An opportunity to study with her was all I really wanted to do before I died, or rather, before she died! And that it was at Miraval, a destination I tempted the universe with by declaring it would forever be out of my league, was the final clue that my time had come. It was as though God sat across from me at my breakfast bar asking if I still wanted to live a life with limits or whether I was finally ready to declare only the best. What would the price have to be to say "no"? Heck, I'd already spent ten thousand dollars on my lawyer's fees. I'd already spent ten thousand on a new deck. I'd already spent ten thousand to repair the basement flood. Ten thousand dollars—okay, that was it! That was the number. Ha.

What a relief it was to find out that the retreat would cost me much less. And I'll tell you, it was worth every penny of it and more!

So what was next now that I had done the only thing I'd ever dreamed of doing for every day since I could remember? Well, I'm reminded of a scene in the kids' Disney movie *Tangled* where Rapunzel waits with Flynn Rider to see the lanterns released from the castle. My memory of their conversation, which I'm paraphrasing here, goes something like this:

"Are you excited?" he asks.

"I'm scared," she replies. "What if it's not like anything I've been dreaming of?"

"But it will be," he assures her.

"And what if it *is* everything I've dreamed of. What will I do then?"

"You'll get a new dream."

Chapter 17

The Last Chapter

Daily Affirmation #17:

**"Everything I need to know is revealed to me
in the perfect time and space sequence."**

As I write this last chapter, I confess I have not written all of the chapters in between. So, how do I know that this is the last chapter? Because the first chapter is about the revelation of the K, C, and T in my license plate, my vanity initials, my middle initials, chosen for me. When I wrote that chapter, I knew I would spend the next few years collecting all the stories in my life that made me recognize the countless ways in which the universe conspires for my success. Writing each chapter realigns me with my perfect birthright to a divinely unfolding life of ever-expanding joy and appreciation. And I knew that when I wrote that first chapter, my book would be complete when the secret behind the 17 in my license plate revealed itself to me. Today is that day.

I have always been a numbers gal. I have spent more than my share of spare time since I was a little girl thinking about digits. They all have a different feel to me, as though each one has its own personality. I excelled so much in math through my entire schooling that I eventually devoted myself to a career of teaching the joy of numbers to others. (Though my high school students' perspectives may differ slightly from my own.) Do you remember the movie *A Beautiful Mind*? I cried when I saw it. No, I sobbed. Now I know why: the connections and the patterns and the dance numbers play out can be so enchanting, so mesmerizing, so engaging, so maddening, so insanely magnificent that sometimes I feel a bit freakish about my passion for digits.

When I got older, I discovered my obsession was validated as the science of numerology, and I dove into studying it headfirst (Pun very much intended here!). To get a basic understanding of the way numerology works, know that everything can be reduced to a single digit between 1 and 9 by finding the sum of all digits. For example, my birthday, March 1, 1975, is an 8, since $3+1+1+9+7+5 = 26$ and $2+6 = 8$, and I was thrilled to find out that the same process works even when no numbers are involved since each letter has its own assigned digit: A is a 1, B is a 2, C is a 3, and so on. So when each letter of my birth name is converted to a digit, the total sum is an 8, but even more fascinating is that when all the vowels in my birth name are added, the sum is also, you guessed it, an 8. Triple jackpot! The Chinese would say that a triple 8 in numerology charts rivals winning the lottery. You could say that 8 is my lucky number. Soooo, the 17 on my plate, which is a numerological 8 since $1+7 = 8$, makes perfect sense.

This, however, was far too obvious to satisfy my curious mind. I heard the questions, "Why not just 8? Why not 26? Why not 35? *Why* 1 and 7?" There has to be a purpose behind that combination, and so the searching and asking continued.

Then this morning, I put together a lesson for my class in which each student coded his or her first name to the assigned digits. We tallied up our results, and everyone left owning his or her personal number. One student lagged behind.

"What was your digit, Paige?" I asked.

"A three," she replied.

Interesting to me was that my next thought was about the P in her name, since the lead letter has a reputation for being a driving force behind our personalities. Then I heard the words "Well, P is a seven, so I guess that makes you some combination of a 3 and a 7, Paige," and I wondered in that moment why I bothered to go more in depth with her (based on the look from her that indicated I cared *way* more about digits than she might ever hope to!).

At the end of the day, before the sun began setting and daily activities settled down once more, the quiet moments revealed the answers to me. In a flash, all the computations came flooding through, and I got it! *I'm* a 1 and a 7! *I* am the 17. The 17 is the one constant in all of the change. *Seema.* I have always been Seema, and that is the constant. "S" is a 1, and S+E+E+M+A = 1+5+5+4+1 = 16 → 1+6 = 7. My first name, my steady name, my "me" in this lifetime and my driving force behind all the changes in the K, the C, and the T, is a combination of a 1 and a 7!

When I look at my license plate now, I know my life is in perfect order. I know my divorce was not a mistake. I know I'm on my chosen path. I know everything is unfolding before me in this time-space reality with divine guidance. I know I am cocreating my life with Life itself and I lose any illusion of fear, knowing I am completely supported by the universe. Someone, something, watches over me. Call it God, call it my higher self, call it angels, call it what you will. I know it is real because I feel it, and now my license plate allows my eyes to see that reality too.

The last thought I have on the whole subject is that my little mind, with all its brilliant functions and capabilities, just does not have the capacity to contrive all this on its own, but it certainly does have the capacity to receive. And that makes me smile. As for the proof that the universe is behind it all? Well, my mind can hardly conceive of any other force great enough to contrive something cleverer. Can yours?

Bonus Chapter

Little Things

Eternal Affirmation:

"All is Well."
—Abraham-Hicks

s you might know, the head of a major company survived the tragedy of 9/11 in New York because his son started kindergarten that morning.

Another fellow was alive because it was his turn to bring donuts.

One woman was late because her alarm clock didn't go off in time.

One was late because of being stuck on the NJ Turnpike because of an auto accident.

One of them missed his bus.

One spilled food on her clothes and had to take time to change.

One's car wouldn't start.

One went back to answer the telephone.

One had a child that dawdled and didn't get ready as soon as he should have.

One couldn't get a taxi.

The one that struck me was the man who put on a new pair of shoes that morning, took the various means to get to work, but before he got there, he developed a blister on his foot. He stopped at a drugstore to buy a Band-Aid. That is why he is alive today.

Now when I am stuck in traffic . . .

miss an elevator . . .

turn back to answer a ringing telephone . . .

all the little things that annoy me . . .

I think to myself . . .

This is exactly where God wants me to be at this very moment.

The next time your morning seems to be going wrong,

the children are slow getting dressed,

you can't seem to find the car keys,

you hit every traffic light . . .

don't get mad or frustrated;

God is at work watching over you.

May God continue to bless you with all those annoying little things—
and may you remember and appreciate their possible purpose.

—Author Unknown, *www.inspirationalstories.com*

Afterword

The Law of Attraction is universal. "Like attracts like." "Birds of a feather flock together." We all have some awareness of it. And when we attract what pleases us, it's easy to take credit for it. I think this is a great place to start examining the events in your life. After all, you are a magnificent creator! Everything that fills you with joy, laughter, enthusiasm, passion, hope, and inspiration is a direct result of the intentions you set forth and the thoughts you contributed to their being present in your life. Since no one else has any power to create your reality, you can be the author of these fantastic creations.

That leads us next to consider the mixed bag of things that aren't quite as we might wish them to be, the things that frustrate, annoy, and diminish our joy. Since no one else has any power to create in your reality, you are also the author of these fantastic creations. My hope is that we'll all learn to take credit for even the things that displease us, as this is where I discovered the source of my own power. When I realized I created everything that showed up in my experience, by the virtue of my magnetic attracting power to all people, places, and experiences that are a direct match to the signal I am broadcasting to the universe, then I began to fine-tune my dial (hence the work with daily affirmations). I even began to find appreciation for those displeasing events, because they revealed to me one more limiting or hindering thought I could begin to shift and release. I imagine sometimes how a life void of negative beliefs might be lived, and I have set course to discover it. As

I began to connect the dots between the thoughts I hear internally and the things I see materializing in my life externally, I no longer felt a victim of anyone or anything. And I eventually stopped blaming others for being the perfect match to what I drew in, when I could be honest enough with myself about what I truly believed.

The Law of Attraction brings us what we believe to be true. Think about that for a moment. Do you believe there won't be good parking at a busy event? The universe will prove to you that it is, if you do. Do you believe you must work long hours to be successful? The universe will set it up just so, if you do. Do you believe holidays can be a stressful time of the year? The universe will arrange all matching circumstances for you, if you do. The good news for me is that beliefs are just thoughts I keep thinking, and my thoughts can be changed. Therefore, shifting my beliefs is possible. So, one thought at a time, I consciously choose thoughts that feel better, exchanging each negative thought for one that serves me better. And slowly over time, I am digging trenches in my mind to direct my life force to flow in the direction of the beliefs that create a life I love to live.

The stories I have shared with you are my personal account of the miraculous and synchronistic ways cooperating components all fell into place when I allowed the universe to have a hand in a situation, and the predictable, determined ways they materialized when my power was focused in ways wanted or unwanted. I open up the personal pages of my own life because in doing the work of connecting the dots between what I was thinking and what I therefore attracted, I have unearthed immeasurable peace, satisfaction, and inspiration as I journey forward. I wrote this book as an invitation to you, the reader, to sift through your own stories and find your own evidence that you are the powerful creator of your life too. It's an indescribable feeling to know unequivocally, beyond a shadow of a doubt, that you are in control. You always have been. And now it's time to take hold of the steering wheel and drive on to the path of your best life.

Acknowledgments

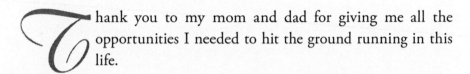hank you to my mom and dad for giving me all the opportunities I needed to hit the ground running in this life.

Thank you to my Jayshree *masi* for her unconditional love and faith in who I am and in what I do.

Thank you to my grandfather, Shanti, for your work from the other side. I wish I had known you in your lifetime here on Earth.

Thank you to my greatest teacher, Dharma, and my steady guide, Devin. You joined me on this journey just when I needed you most.

Thank you to Sandy for being the twenty-first opinion on every topic!

Thank you to Nancy for being my inspiration as I look forward down my path. Your life is my evidence that anything I desire is possible.

Thank you to Matthew-Lee for inspiring me to share my stories.

Thank you to Yashoda for being a divine instrument of God.

Thank you to Lon for literally and figuratively helping me to rebuild this life I love to live so much!

Thank you to Sean for making it possible for me to heal all that longed to be whole.

Thank you to Mark for initiating the process of remembering who I really am.

Thank you to Mara for the perpetual reminder to "just notice."

Thank you to Kristen for lending me your tapes so I could learn how to rewrite mine.

Thank you to Anna Maria for being there when I woke up in a strange new place and for being such a knowledgeable tour guide along the way.

Thank you to Yvette for creating a shift in my life by simply asking me to list ten things I appreciate. With practice, the task has gone from taking all day to complete to being done before my feet even touch the ground each morning!

Thank you to Louise Hay for teaching me how to select just the right words for everything I intend to say.

Thank you to Abraham and Jerry and Esther Hicks for teaching me the rules of the game. Life is so much easier (and more joyful) to play when I know how it works!

Thank you to all my students and colleagues for being my blessed indicators of alignment. You steer me along my path.

Thank you to all the beautiful beings of light who have helped me to polish mine even brighter and brighter. You know who you are!

And thank you to you, my reader. You complete the cycle from which these words were born.

I love you all!

Recommended Reading

Abraham, Esther Hicks, and Jerry Hicks. *Ask and It Is Given: Learning to Manifest Your Desires*. Carlsbad, CA: Hay House, 2004.

Choquette, Sonia. *Trust Your Vibes: Secret Tools for Six-sensory Living*. Carlsbad, CA: Hay House, 2004.

Dyer, Wayne W. *Excuses Begone!: How to Change Lifelong, Self-defeating Thinking Habits*. Carlsbad, CA: Hay House, 2009.

Emoto, Masaru. *The Hidden Messages in Water*. Hillsboro, OR: Beyond Words Publishing, 2004.

Frankl, Viktor E. *Man's Search for Meaning*. Boston: Beacon Press, 2006.

Gawain, Shakti. *Creative Visualization: Use the Power of Your Imagination to Create What You Want in Your Life*. Rev. ed. San Rafael, Calif.: New World Library, 1995.

Hay, Louise L. *You Can Heal Your Life*. Carlsbad, CA: Hay House, 2008.

Katie, Byron, and Stephen Mitchell. *Loving What Is: Four Questions That Can Change Your Life*. New York: Harmony, 2002.

Myss, Caroline M. *Anatomy of the Spirit: The Seven Stages of Power and Healing*. New York: Harmony, 1996.

Roberts, Jane. *Seth Speaks: The Eternal Validity of the Soul.* Englewood Cliffs, N.J.: Prentice-Hall, 1972.

Shinn, Florence Scovel. *The Game of Life and How to Play It.* Marina del Rey, Calif.: DeVorss, 1925.

Virtue, Doreen. *Healing with the Angels: How the Angels Can Assist You in Every Area of Your Life.* Carlsbad, CA: Hay House, 1999.

Recommended Viewing

Cox, Courtney, Keri Russell, Adam Sandler, et al. *Bedtime Stories*, DVD. Directed by Andrew Gunn. Walt Disney Studios Home Entertainment, 2009.

MacDowell, Andie, Bill Murray, et al. *Groundhog Day*, DVD. Directed by Harold Ramis. Columbia Pictures, 1993.

Bening, Annette, Paul Dano, Zoe Kazan, et al. *Ruby Sparks*, DVD. Directed by Jonathan Dayton. Twentieth Century Fox Home Entertainment, 2012.

Fishburne, Laurence, Carrie-Anne Moss, Keanu Reeves, et al. *The Matrix*, DVD. Directed by Andy Wachowski. Warner Bros. Pictures, 1999.

Beckwith, Michael, Jack Canfield, John Gray, Neale Donald Walsch, et al. *The Secret*, DVD. Directed by Rhonda Byrne. TS Production LLC, 2006.

Bailey, Jr., Robert, John Ross Bowie, Elaine Hendrix, Marlee Matlin, Barry Newman, Armin Shimerman, et al. *What the #$*! Do We (K)now!?*, DVD. Directed by Mark Vicente. 20th Century Fox Home Entertainment, 2004.

Braden, Gregg, Louise Hay, Esther Hicks, Suzanne Keilly, Cheryl Richardson, et al. *You Can Heal Your Life*, DVD. Directed by Louise L. Hay. Hay House, 2007.

CPSIA information can be obtained at www.ICGtesting.com
Printed in the USA
LVOW080024210613

339563LV00004B/10/P